MY THOUGHTS & Feelings JOURNAL

MY journal

Date: 9th july

My Mood Tracker

Sleepy Time

I slept from

....8.30..... PM

......7.00... AM

Happy Thoughts

I felt happy today when:

I went out on my bike after school!

Today, I want to remember.....

The really cool rainbow I saw today - that took up the whole sky!

Positivity
Positive thoughts for today:

I am AWESOME

I am KIND

I can really DANCE!

MY GOALS!
1) art homework ✓
2) chapter of book ✓
3) tiday room ✓
4) practice dance ✓

EXAMPLE

KEEPING ACTIVE!
Exercise completed today?

I did ...... Bike ride! ...

For ..... 30 ... minutes

Gratitude Today I'm grateful for:
1) ......My lovely Cat!......
2) ......My best friend Lucy......
3) ......My new book......

MY journal

Date:

My Mood Tracker

I felt happy today when:

....

....

....

HAPPY THOUGHTS

Today, I want to remember.....

....

....

....

Positivity
Positive thoughts for today:

MY GOALS!

1) _____
2) _____
3) _____
4) _____

KEEPING ACTIVE!
Exercise completed today?

I did ....

For .... minutes

Gratitude Today I'm grateful for:

1) ....
2) ....
3) ....

MY journal

Date: _____

My Mood Tracker

Sleepy Time

I Slept from

.... PM

.... AM

Some feelings I've felt today are:

....

....

....

you are ENOUGH

Something Kind I did Today was:

....

....

....

FUNNY

Funny thoughts I've had today:

Cool stuff I want to do:

1) _____

2) _____

3) _____

4) _____

Take Notice!

Something beautiful I saw today was....

....

....

Giving thanks Today I'm thankful that...

1) ....

2) ....

3) ....

MY journal

Date:

Sleepy Time

I Slept from

.... PM

.... AM

I felt proud today when:

....

....

....

Something interesting that happened today was:

....

....

....

Kindness

kind things that I have done today!

Things that made me happy today:

1) _____

2) _____

3) _____

4) _____

Keep Dreaming

If I could have done ANYTHING today, what would it have been?

....

....

My Plans 3 things I need to do tomorrow:

1) ....

2) ....

3) ....

MY journal

Date:

My Mood Tracker

Sleepy Time

I Slept from

.... PM

.... AM

Key emotions I've felt today:

....

....

....

YES you can!

Something I enjoyed about today was:

....

....

....

Laughter

Some things that made me laugh today...

Four things that made today great!

1) _____

2) _____

3) _____

4) _____

Keep Smiling

I felt GOOD today when:

....

....

....

People 3 people that were kind to me today:

1) ....

2) ....

3) ....

MY journal

Date:

My Mood Tracker

Sleepy Time

I slept from

.... PM

.... AM

Any worries? Share here!

....

....

....

Something I've been thinking a lot about is....

....

....

....

fun

Some things that made today fun...

Things I want to do TOMORROW:

1) _____

2) _____

3) _____

4) _____

friendship

I was a good friend today to....

....

....

....

Today   An important thing that happened was....

....

....

....

MY journal Date:

My Mood Tracker

Sleepy Time

I Slept from

.... PM

.... AM

Journal Entry - Write Anything!

....

....

....

....

....

....

....

....

....

Free Space/Doodle!

MY journal Date:

Sleepy Time
I Slept from
.... PM
.... AM

I felt great today when....

....

....

....

Something that could have been better today was....

....

....

....

Thoughts

Some things I have thought about today:

Confidence

I did well today when...

....
....
....

DOODLE SPACE

MY DAY

3 words to describe my day:

1) ....
2) ....
3) ....

MY journal

Date:

My Mood Tracker

Sleepy Time

I Slept from

.... PM

.... AM

I felt happy today when:

....

....

....

HAPPY THOUGHTS

Today, I want to remember.....

....

....

....

Positivity
Positive thoughts for today:

KEEPING ACTIVE!
Exercise completed today?

I did ....

For .... minutes

Gratitude Today I'm grateful for:

1) ....

2) ....

3) ....

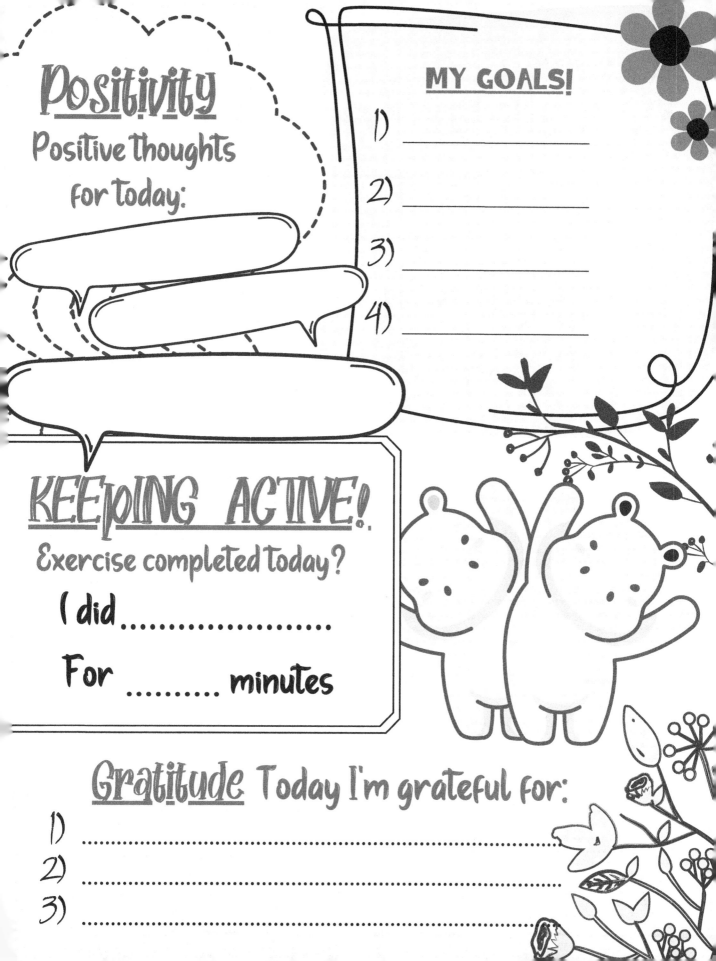

MY journal Date:

My Mood Tracker

Sleepy Time

I Slept from

.... PM

.... AM

Some feelings I've felt today are:

....

....

....

you are ENOUGH

Something kind I did today was:

....

....

....

FUNNY

Funny thoughts I've had Today:

Cool stuff I want to do:

1) _____

2) _____

3) _____

4) _____

Take Notice!

Something beautiful I saw Today was....

....

....

Giving thanks Today I'm thankful that...

1) ....

2) ....

3) ....

MY journal

Date:

My Mood Tracker

I felt proud today when:

....

....

....

Sleepy Time

I Slept from

.... PM

.... AM

Something interesting that happened today was:

....

....

....

Kindness

Kind things that I have done today!

Things that made me happy today:

1) _____

2) _____

3) _____

4) _____

Keep Dreaming

If I could have done ANYTHING today, what would it have been?

....

....

My Plans 3 things I need to do tomorrow:

1) ....

2) ....

3) ....

MY journal

Date:

My Mood Tracker

Sleepy Time

I Slept from

.... PM

.... AM

Key emotions I've felt today:

....

....

....

YES
you can!

Something I enjoyed about today was:

....

....

....

Laughter

Some things that
made me laugh today...

Four things that made today great!

1) _____

2) _____

3) _____

4) _____

Keep Smiling

I felt GOOD today when:

....

....

....

People 3 people that were kind to me today:

1) ....

2) ....

3) ....

MY journal

Date:

My Mood Tracker

Sleepy Time

I Slept from

.... PM

.... AM

Any worries? Share here!

....

....

....

Something I've been thinking a lot about is....

....

....

....

fun

Some things that
made today fun...

1) _____

2) _____

3) _____

4) _____

friendship

I was a good friend today to....

....

....

....

Today

An important thing that happened was....

....

....

....

MY journal

Date:

My Mood Tracker

Sleepy Time

I Slept from

.... PM

.... AM

Journal Entry - Write Anything!

....

....

....

....

....

....

....

....

....

Free Space/Doodle!

MY journal

Date:

My Mood Tracker

Sleepy Time

I Slept from

.... PM

.... AM

I felt great Today when....

....

....

....

Something That could have been better today was....

....

....

....

Thoughts

Some things I have thought about today:

DOODLE SPACE

Confidence

I did well today when...

....

....

....

MY DAY

3 words to describe my day:

1) ....

2) ....

3) ....

MY Journal

Date:

My Mood Tracker

Sleepy Time

I Slept from

.... PM

.... AM

I felt happy today when:

....

....

HAPPY THOUGHTS

Today, I want to remember.....

....

....

....

Positivity
Positive thoughts for today:

MY GOALS!
1) _____
2) _____
3) _____
4) _____

KEEPING ACTIVE!
Exercise completed today?

I did ....

For .... minutes

Gratitude Today I'm grateful for:
1) ....
2) ....
3) ....

MY journal

Date:

My Mood Tracker

Some feelings I've felt today are:

....

....

....

you are
ENOUGH

Something Kind I did today was:

....

....

....

FUNNY

Funny thoughts I've had today:

Cool stuff I want to do:

1) _____

2) _____

3) _____

4) _____

Take Notice!

Something beautiful I saw today was....

....

....

Giving thanks Today I'm thankful that...

1) ....

2) ....

3) ....

MY journal

Date:

My Mood Tracker

Sleepy Time

I Slept from

.... PM

.... AM

I felt proud today when:

....

....

....

Something interesting that happened today was:

....

....

....

Kindness

Kind things that I have done today!

Things that made me happy today:

1) _____

2) _____

3) _____

4) _____

Keep Dreaming

If I could have done ANYTHING today, what would it have been?

....

....

My Plans 3 things I need to do tomorrow:

1) ....

2) ....

3) ....

MY journal

Date:

My Mood Tracker

Key emotions I've felt today:

....

....

....

YES you can!

Something I enjoyed about today was:

....

....

....

Laughter

Some things that made me laugh today...

Four things that made today great!

1) _____

2) _____

3) _____

4) _____

Keep Smiling

I felt GOOD today when:

....

....

....

People   3 people that were kind to me today:

1) ....

2) ....

3) ....

MY journal

Date:

My Mood Tracker

Any worries? Share here!

....

....

....

Something I've been thinking a lot about is....

....

....

....

fun

Some things that made today fun...

Things I want to do TOMORROW:

1) _____

2) _____

3) _____

4) _____

friendship

I was a good friend today to....

....

....

....

Today   An important thing that happened was....

....

....

....

MY journal Date:

My Mood Tracker

Journal Entry - Write Anything!

....

....

....

....

....

....

....

....

....

Free Space/Doodle!

MY journal

Date:

Sleepy Time

I slept from

.... PM

.... AM

I felt great today when....

....

....

....

Something that could have been better today was....

....

....

....

Thoughts

Some things I have thought about today:

DOODLE SPACE

Confidence

I did well today when...

....
....
....

MY DAY   3 words to describe my day:

1) ....
2) ....
3) ....

MY journal

Date:

My Mood Tracker

Sleepy Time

I Slept from

.... PM

.... AM

I felt happy today when:

....

....

....

HAPPY THOUGHTS

Today, I want to remember.....

....

....

....

Positivity
Positive thoughts for today:

MY GOALS!

1) _____

2) _____

3) _____

4) _____

KEEpING ACTIVE!
Exercise completed today?

I did ....

For .... minutes

Gratitude Today I'm grateful for:

1) ....

2) ....

3) ....

MY journal

Date:

My Mood Tracker

Sleepy Time

I Slept from

.... PM

.... AM

Some feelings I've felt today are:

....

....

....

you are ENOUGH

Something Kind I did today was:

....

....

....

FUNNY

Funny thoughts I've had today:

Cool stuff I want to do:

1) _____

2) _____

3) _____

4) _____

Take Notice!

Something beautiful I saw today was....

....

....

Giving thanks Today I'm thankful that...

1) ....

2) ....

3) ....

MY journal

Date:

My Mood Tracker

Sleepy Time

I Slept from

.... PM

.... AM

I felt proud today when:

....

....

....

Something interesting that happened today was:

....

....

....

Kindness

Kind things that I have done today!

Things that made me happy today:

1) _____

2) _____

3) _____

4) _____

Keep Dreaming

If I could have done ANYTHING today, what would it have been?

....

....

My Plans 3 things I need to do tomorrow:

1) ....

2) ....

3) ....

MY journal

Date:

My Mood Tracker

Key emotions I've felt today:

....

....

....

YES
you can!

Something I enjoyed about today was:

....

....

....

Laughter

Some things that made me laugh today...

Four things that made today great!

1) _____

2) _____

3) _____

4) _____

Keep Smiling

I felt GOOD today when:

....

....

....

People 3 people that were kind to me today:

1) ....

2) ....

3) ....

MY journal

Date:

My Mood Tracker

Sleepy Time

I slept from

.... PM

.... AM

Any worries? Share here!

....

....

....

Something I've been thinking a lot about is....

....

....

....

fun

Some things that made today fun...

1) _____

2) _____

3) _____

4) _____

friendship

I was a good friend today to....

....

....

....

Today   An important thing that happened was....

....

....

....

MY journal

Date:

My Mood Tracker

Sleepy Time
I Slept from

.... PM

.... AM

Journal Entry - Write Anything!

....

....

....

....

....

....

....

....

....

Free Space/Doodle!

MY journal

Date:

My Mood Tracker

I felt great today when....

....

....

....

Sleepy Time

I Slept from

.... PM

.... AM

Something that could have been better today was....

....

....

....

Thoughts

Some things I have thought about today:

DOODLE SPACE

Confidence

I did well today when...

....

....

....

MY DAY

3 words to describe my day:

1) ....

2) ....

3) ....

MY journal

Date:

My Mood Tracker

I felt happy today when:

....

....

....

HAPPY THOUGHTS

Today, I want to remember.....

....

....

....

Positivity
Positive thoughts for today:

MY GOALS!
1) _____
2) _____
3) _____
4) _____

KEEPING ACTIVE!
Exercise completed today?

I did.........................

For .... minutes

Gratitude Today I'm grateful for:
1) ....
2) ....
3) ....

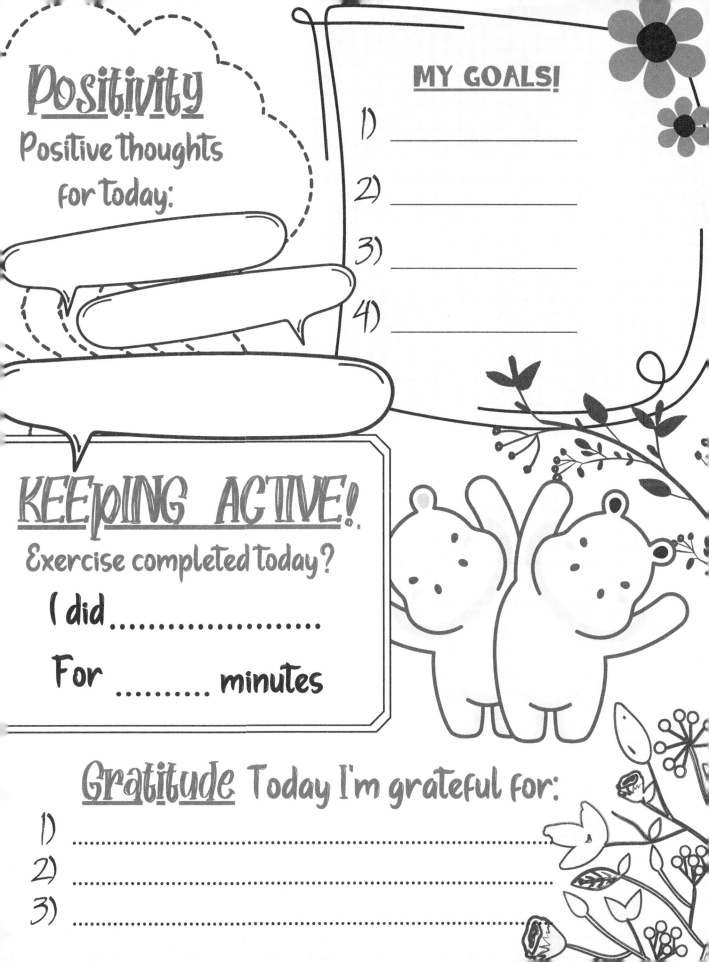

MY journal

Date:

My Mood Tracker

Sleepy Time

I Slept from

.... PM

.... AM

Some feelings I've felt today are:

....

....

....

you are ENOUGH

Something kind I did today was:

....

....

....

FUNNY

Funny thoughts I've had today:

Cool stuff I want to do:

1) _____

2) _____

3) _____

4) _____

Take Notice!

Something beautiful I saw today was....

....

....

Giving thanks Today I'm thankful that...

1) ....

2) ....

3) ....

MY journal

Date:

My Mood Tracker

Sleepy Time

I Slept from

.... PM

.... AM

I felt proud today when:

....

....

....

Something interesting that happened today was:

....

....

....

Kindness

Kind things that I have done today!

Keep Dreaming

If I could have done ANYTHING today, what would it have been?

....

....

My Plans 3 things I need to do tomorrow:

1) ....
2) ....
3) ....

Things that made me happy today:

1) _____

2) _____

3) _____

4) _____

MY journal

Date:

My Mood Tracker

I Slept from

.... PM

.... AM

Key emotions I've felt today:

....

....

....

YES
you can!

Something I enjoyed about today was:

....

....

....

Laughter

Some things that made me laugh today...

Four things that made today great!

1) _____

2) _____

3) _____

4) _____

Keep Smiling

I felt GOOD today when:

....

....

....

People 3 people that were kind to me today:

1) ....

2) ....

3) ....

MY journal

Date:

My Mood Tracker

Sleepy Time

I Slept from

.... PM

.... AM

Any worries? Share here!

....

....

....

Something I've been thinking a lot about is....

....

....

....

fun

Some things that made today fun...

Things I want to do TOMORROW:

1) _____

2) _____

3) _____

4) _____

friendship

I was a good friend today to....

....

....

....

Today   An important thing that happened was....

....

....

....

MY journal

Date:

My Mood Tracker

I Slept from

.... PM

.... AM

Journal Entry - Write Anything!

....

....

....

....

....

....

....

....

....

....

free Space/Doodle!

MY journal

Date:

My Mood Tracker

Sleepy Time

I Slept from

.... PM

.... AM

I felt great today when....

....

....

....

Something that could have been better today was....

....

....

....

Thoughts

Some things I have thought about today:

DOODLE SPACE

Confidence

I did well today when...

....

....

....

MY DAY

3 words to describe my day:

1) ....

2) ....

3) ....

MY journal

Date:

My Mood Tracker

Sleepy Time

I Slept from

.... PM

.... AM

I felt happy today when:

....

....

....

HAPPY THOUGHTS

Today, I want to remember.....

....

....

....

Positivity
Positive thoughts for today:

MY GOALS!
1) _____
2) _____
3) _____
4) _____

KEEPING ACTIVE!
Exercise completed today?

I did..........................

For .... minutes

Gratitude Today I'm grateful for:
1) ....
2) ....
3) ....

MY journal

Date:

My Mood Tracker

Sleepy Time

I Slept from

.... PM

.... AM

Some feelings I've felt today are:

....

....

....

you are ENOUGH

Something kind I did today was:

....

....

....

FUNNY

Funny thoughts I've had today:

Cool stuff I want to do:

1) _____

2) _____

3) _____

4) _____

Take Notice!

Something beautiful I saw today was....

....

....

Giving thanks Today I'm thankful that...

1) ....

2) ....

3) ....

MY journal Date:

My Mood Tracker

Sleepy Time

I slept from

.... PM

.... AM

I felt proud today when:

....

....

....

Something interesting that happened today was:

....

....

....

Kindness

Kind things that I have done today!

Keep Dreaming

If I could have done ANYTHING today, what would it have been?

....

....

My Plans 3 things I need to do tomorrow:

1) ....

2) ....

3) ....

Things that made me happy today:

1) _____

2) _____

3) _____

4) _____

MY journal

Date:

My Mood Tracker

Sleepy Time

I slept from

.... PM

.... AM

Key emotions I've felt today:

....

....

....

YES you can!

Something I enjoyed about today was:

....

....

....

Laughter

Some things that made me laugh today...

Four things that made today great!

1) _____

2) _____

3) _____

4) _____

Keep Smiling

I felt GOOD today when:

....

....

....

People 3 people that were kind to me today:

1) ....

2) ....

3) ....

MY journal

Date:

My Mood Tracker

Sleepy Time

I Slept from

.... PM

.... AM

Any worries? Share here!

....

....

....

Something I've been thinking a lot about is....

....

....

....

fun

Some things that made today fun...

Things I want to do TOMORROW:

1) _____

2) _____

3) _____

4) _____

friendship

I was a good friend today to....

....

....

....

Today   An important thing that happened was....

....

....

....

MY journal

Date:

My Mood Tracker

Sleepy Time

I Slept from

.... PM

.... AM

Journal Entry - Write Anything!

....

....

....

....

....

....

....

....

....

....

Free Space/Doodle!

MY journal

Date:

My Mood Tracker

Sleepy Time

I Slept from

.... PM

.... AM

I felt great today when....

....

....

....

Something that could have been better today was....

....

....

....

Thoughts

Some things I have thought about today:

DOODLE SPACE

Confidence

I did well today when...

....

....

....

MY DAY   3 words to describe my day:

1) ....

2) ....

3) ....

MY journal

Date:

My Mood Tracker

I felt happy today when:

....

....

HAPPY THOUGHTS

Today, I want to remember.....

....

....

....

Positivity

Positive thoughts for today:

MY GOALS!

1) _____

2) _____

3) _____

4) _____

KEEPING ACTIVE!

Exercise completed today?

I did ....

For .... minutes

Gratitude Today I'm grateful for:

1) ....

2) ....

3) ....

MY journal

Date:

My Mood Tracker

Some feelings I've felt today are:

....

....

....

you are ENOUGH

Something kind I did today was:

....

....

....

FUNNY

Funny thoughts I've had today:

Cool stuff I want to do:

1) _____

2) _____

3) _____

4) _____

Take Notice!

Something beautiful I saw today was....

....

....

Giving thanks Today I'm thankful that...

1) ....

2) ....

3) ....

MY journal

Date:

My Mood Tracker

I felt proud today when:

....

....

....

Sleepy Time

I Slept from

.... PM

.... AM

Something interesting that happened today was:

....

....

....

Kindness

Kind things that I have done today!

Things that made me happy today:

1) _____

2) _____

3) _____

4) _____

Keep Dreaming

If I could have done ANYTHING today, what would it have been?

....

....

My Plans 3 things I need to do tomorrow:

1) ....

2) ....

3) ....

MY journal

Date:

My Mood Tracker

Key emotions I've felt today:

....

....

....

YES
you can!

Something I enjoyed about today was:

....

....

....

Laughter

Some things that
made me laugh today...

Four things that made today great!

1) _____

2) _____

3) _____

4) _____

Keep Smiling

I felt GOOD today when:

....

....

....

People   3 people that were kind to me today:

1) ....

2) ....

3) ....

MY journal

Date:

My Mood Tracker

Sleepy Time

I Slept from

.... PM

.... AM

Any worries? Share here!

....

....

....

Something I've been thinking a lot about is....

....

....

....

fun

Some things that made today fun...

Things I want to do TOMORROW:

1) _____
2) _____
3) _____
4) _____

Friendship

I was a good friend today to....

....
....
....

Today   An important thing that happened was....

....
....
....

MY journal

Date:

My Mood Tracker

Sleepy Time

I Slept from

.... PM

.... AM

Journal Entry - Write Anything!

....

....

....

....

....

....

....

....

....

....

Free Space/Doodle!

MY journal

Date:

My Mood Tracker

I felt great today when....

....

....

....

Something that could have been better today was....

....

....

....

Thoughts

Some things I have thought about today:

DOODLE SPACE

Confidence

I did well today when...

....
....
....

MY DAY   3 words to describe my day:

1) ....
2) ....
3) ....

MY journal

Date:

My Mood Tracker

Sleepy Time

I Slept from

.... PM

.... AM

I felt happy today when:

....

....

HAPPY THOUGHTS

Today, I want to remember.....

....

....

....

Positivity
Positive thoughts for today:

MY GOALS!
1) _____
2) _____
3) _____
4) _____

KEEPING ACTIVE!
Exercise completed today?

I did ....

For .... minutes

Gratitude Today I'm grateful for:
1) ....
2) ....
3) ....

MY journal

Date:

My Mood Tracker

Sleepy Time

I Slept from

.... PM

.... AM

Some feelings I've felt today are:

....

....

....

you are ENOUGH

Something kind I did today was:

....

....

....

FUNNY

Funny thoughts I've had today:

Cool stuff I want to do:

1) _____

2) _____

3) _____

4) _____

Take Notice!

Something beautiful I saw today was....

....

....

Giving thanks Today I'm thankful that...

1) ....

2) ....

3) ....

MY journal

Date:

My Mood Tracker

Sleepy Time

I Slept from

.... PM

.... AM

I felt proud today when:

....

....

....

Something interesting that happened today was:

....

....

....

Kindness

kind things that I have done today!

Things that made me happy today:

1) _____

2) _____

3) _____

4) _____

Keep Dreaming

If I could have done ANYTHING today, what would it have been?

....

....

My Plans 3 things I need to do tomorrow:

1) ....

2) ....

3) ....

MY journal

Date:

My Mood Tracker

Key emotions I've felt today:

....

....

....

YES you can!

Something I enjoyed about today was:

....

....

....

Laughter

Some things that made me laugh today...

Four things that made today great!

1) _____
2) _____
3) _____
4) _____

Keep Smiling

I felt GOOD today when:

....
....
....

People 3 people that were kind to me today:

1) ....
2) ....
3) ....

MY journal

Date:

My Mood Tracker

Sleepy Time

I Slept from

.... PM

.... AM

Any worries? Share here!

....

....

....

Something I've been thinking a lot about is....

....

....

....

fun

Some things that
made today fun...

1) _____

2) _____

3) _____

4) _____

friendship

I was a good friend today to....

....

....

....

Today   An important thing that happened was....

....

....

....

MY journal

Date:

My Mood Tracker

Sleepy Time

I Slept from

.... PM

.... AM

Journal Entry - Write Anything!

....

....

....

....

....

....

....

....

....

Free Space/Doodle!

MY journal

Date:

My Mood Tracker

Sleepy Time

I slept from

.... PM

.... AM

I felt great today when....

....

....

....

Something that could have been better today was....

....

....

....

Thoughts

Some things I have thought about today:

DOODLE SPACE

Confidence

I did well today when...

....

....

....

MY DAY 3 words to describe my day:

1) ....

2) ....

3) ....

Made in the USA
Las Vegas, NV
07 September 2023

77176599R00066